Words from Jesus

by Sarah Jarvis

First published 2010. Copyright © 2010
Autumn House Publishing (Europe) Ltd.

British Library Cataloguing in Publication Data. A catalogue
record for this book is available from the British Library.
ISBN 978-1-906381-70-7
Published by Autumn House, Grantham, Lincolnshire.
Designed by Abigail Murphy
Printed in Thailand.

Unless otherwise indicated, Scripture references are taken
from the *New International Version* of the Bible.
Other versions used, indicated by initials:
MGE = *The Message* (NavPress)
NKJV = *New King James Version* (Thomas Nelson)
NLT = *New Living Translation* (Tyndale)

Jesus, the One and Only

'I am the way and the truth and the life.'
John 14:6

Believe in Jesus, the Truth, and he
will show you the way to life everlasting.

His invitation

'Come, follow me.'
Matthew 4:19

It makes sense to follow the only
one who knows the way.

The guiding principle of his conduct . . .

'It is written . . .'
Matthew 4:4

If you want to follow Jesus, the Way,
then make his Word the guiding
principle of *your* conduct, too.

The only source of lasting nourishment

'Jesus answered, It is written: "Man does not live on bread alone, but on every word that comes from the mouth of God." '

Matthew 4:4

Feeding daily on the Word will keep you in good spiritual health.

Hungry?

*'I am the bread of life. He who comes
to me will never go hungry.'*

John 6:35

Only Jesus can satisfy. Go to him for
your daily sustenance of food for the soul.

Thirsty?

'Whoever drinks the water I give him will never thirst. Indeed, the water I give him will become in him a spring of water welling up to eternal life.'

John 4:14

Drink the living water and your
eternal destiny is secure.

The guiding light

'I am the light of the world. Whoever follows me will never walk in darkness, but will have the light of life.'

John 8:12

Why stumble about in the dark when there's a source of light to help you see your way home?

Lights in the darkness

'You are the light of the world. . . . let your light shine before men, that they may see your good deeds and praise your Father in heaven.'

Matthew 5:14, 16

Jesus, the Light, asks *you* to be a beacon of light in a dark world, leading men to him.

If you want a fruitful life . . .

*'I am the true vine, . . . Remain in me, and
I will remain in you. No branch can bear fruit by
itself; it must remain in the vine. Neither can
you bear fruit unless you remain in me.'*

John 15:1, 4

Stay grafted to the vine.

How much can you manage on your own?

'Apart from me you can do nothing.'
John 15:5

So why try to cope without him?

Jesus, the source of true happiness

'I have told you this so that my joy may be in you and that your joy may be complete.'

John 15:11

Only he can give you lasting fullness of joy.

Eight secrets of true happiness

1. When you realise your need . . .

'You're blessed when you're at the end of your rope. With less of you there is more of God and his rule.'
Matthew 5:3, MGE

. . . God will have the first place in your life that he deserves.

2. When you have cause to mourn

'You're blessed when you feel you've lost what is most dear to you. Only then can you be embraced by the One most dear to you.'
Matthew 5:4, MGE

The One who loves you more than anyone else can comfort you like no one else.

3. True riches

*'You're blessed when you're content with
just who you are – no more, no less. That's
the moment you find yourselves proud owners
of everything that can't be bought.'*
Matthew 5:5, MGE

The wealth of God's Kingdom is
yours for the asking.

4. Hungry and thirsty?

'You're blessed when you've worked up a good appetite for God. He's food and drink in the best meal you'll ever eat.'

Matthew 5:6, MGE

If you hunger and thirst after the right things – the things of God – you'll never be hungry and thirsty.

5. Show you care . . .

*'You're blessed when you care. At the
moment of being "care-full", you
find yourselves cared for.'*
Matthew 5:7, MGE

. . . because God cares for you
more than you'll ever know.

6. Pure in heart?

'You're blessed when you get your inside world – your mind and heart – put right. Then you can see God in the outside world.'
Matthew 5:8, MGE

And you're promised the privilege of meeting him and dwelling with him when he returns.

7. Be a peacemaker

'You're blessed when you can show people how to co-operate instead of compete or fight. That's when you discover who you really are, and your place in God's family.'
Matthew 5:9, MGE

Yes, you'll be accepted as a child of God.

8. When you meet with resistance . . .

'You're blessed when your commitment to God provokes persecution. The persecution drives you even deeper into God's kingdom.'
Matthew 5:10, MGE

. . . be glad about it, because you know you're doing what God requires.

Jesus didn't promise it would be easy

'Enter through the narrow gate. For wide is the gate and broad is the road that leads to destruction, and many enter through it. But small is the gate and narrow the road that leads to life, and only a few find it.'

Matthew 7:13-14

But it's worth the effort as the prize is out of this world!

Being a Christian won't mean winning popularity contests

'If the world hates you, keep in mind that it hated me first. If you belonged to the world, it would love you as its own. As it is, you do not belong to the world, but I have chosen you out of the world. That is why the world hates you.'

John 15:18, 19

The world is fickle, but Jesus' love endures to the end.

Effort is required

'The kingdom of heaven is like treasure hidden in a field. When a man found it, he hid it again, and then in his joy went and sold all he had and bought that field.'

Matthew 13:44

So start digging!

Self-sacrifice is a prerequisite

*'And anyone who does not carry his cross
and follow me cannot be my disciple. . . .
any of you who does not give up everything
he has cannot be my disciple.'*

Luke 14:27, 33

Too much to ask? Tempted to complain?
If you think it's tough, remember he gave up
Heaven and walked to Calvary for you.

Requirement for entry into God's Kingdom

'I tell you the truth, no one can see the kingdom of God unless he is born again.'

John 3:3

Leave behind the old you and let God give you a divine makeover.

One of life's paradoxes

'If anyone would come after me, he must deny himself and take up his cross and follow me. For whoever wants to save his life will lose it, but whoever loses his life for me will find it.'

Matthew 16:24-25

Give up everything that doesn't matter to gain the one thing that does.

Profit or loss?

'What good will it be for a man if he gains the whole world, yet forfeits his soul?'
Matthew 16:26

What the world offers is fleeting.
What Jesus offers is eternal.

The first and greatest commandment

'Love the Lord your God with all your heart and with all your soul and with all your mind.'

Matthew 22:37

Only wholehearted love will do.

And the second commandment

'Love your neighbour as yourself.'
Matthew 22:39

Be proactive in your dealings with others, treating them as you would wish them to treat you.

Get your priorities straight

'Do not store up for yourselves treasures on earth, where moth and rust destroy, and where thieves break in and steal. But store up for yourselves treasures in heaven, where moth and rust do not destroy, and where thieves do not break in and steal. For where your treasure is, there your heart will be also.'

Matthew 6:19-21

Where is *your* treasure stored?

Food with no sell-by date

'Don't waste your energy striving for perishable food like that. Work for the food that sticks with you, food that nourishes your lasting life, food the Son of Man provides. He and what he does are guaranteed by God the Father to last.'

John 6:27, MGE

What God offers is imperishable.

Either/or – not both

'No one can serve two masters. Either he will hate the one and love the other, or he will be devoted to the one and despise the other. You cannot serve both God and Money.'

Matthew 6:24

Who do you want to be *your* Lord?

A bank you can bank on

'Be generous. Give to the poor. Get yourselves a bank that can't go bankrupt, a bank in heaven far from bank robbers, safe from embezzlers, a bank you can bank on.'
Luke 12:33, MGE

Are your investments in the right bank?

The pearl of great price

'Again, the kingdom of heaven is like a merchant looking for fine pearls. When he found one of great value, he went away and sold everything he had and bought it.'
Matthew 13:45, 46

You might have to make sacrifices for the sake of the Kingdom, but you'll be storing up incorruptible treasure in your heavenly bank account.

Cast your bread upon the waters . . .

'Give, and it will be given to you. A good measure, pressed down, shaken together and running over, will be poured into your lap. For with the measure you use, it will be measured to you.'

Luke 6:38

There's joy in generosity – and you'll also learn about the boomerang effect of giving.

Don't worry about a thing

'So do not worry, saying, "What shall we eat?" or "What shall we drink?" or "What shall we wear?" For the pagans run after all these things, and your heavenly Father knows that you need them.'

Matthew 6:31-32

Temporal concerns mustn't consume your thinking.

Prioritise!

'But seek first his kingdom and his righteousness, and all these things will be given to you as well.'
Matthew 6:33

All these things are guaranteed – so why worry about them?

Worrying is futile

'Who of you by worrying can add a single hour to his life? And why do you worry about clothes? See how the lilies of the field grow. They do not labour or spin. Yet I tell you that not even Solomon in all his splendour was dressed like one of these. If that is how God clothes the grass of the field, which is here today and tomorrow is thrown into the fire, will he not much more clothe you, O you of little faith?'

Matthew 6:27-30

Jesus invites us to trust him to supply all our needs.

Our abundantly generous God

'Which of you, if his son asks for bread, will give him a stone? Or if he asks for a fish, will give him a snake? If you, then, though you are evil, know how to give good gifts to your children, how much more will your Father in heaven give good gifts to those who ask him!'

Matthew 7:9-11

God is waiting with arms outstretched to bless those who ask of him.

First things first!

'Martha, Martha, the Lord answered, you are worried and upset about many things, but only one thing is needed. Mary has chosen what is better, and it will not be taken away from her.'

Luke 10:41, 42

Make sure Jesus is your number one concern.

Do you consider yourself to be his friend?

'You are my friends if you do what I command.'
John 15:14

Then do as he asks.

If you want Jesus to dwell in your heart . . .

'Jesus replied, If anyone loves me, he will obey my teaching. My Father will love him, and we will come to him and make our home with him.'

John 14:23

. . . then listen to him and keep his words.

A member of the family?

'For whoever does the will of my Father in heaven is my brother and sister and mother.'
Matthew 12:50

Does your conduct show which family you belong to?

The Law stands!

*'The sky will disintegrate and the
earth dissolve before a single letter
of God's Law wears out.'*
Luke 16:17, MGE

So that means obedience is still required.

Obedience begets love?

'If you obey my commands, you will remain in my love, just as I have obeyed my Father's commands and remain in his love.'

John 15:10

It worked for Jesus, so it'll work for you.

Obedience matters

'If you abide in My word, you are My disciples indeed.'
John 8:31, NKJV

It's the mark of the true disciple.

Obedience = happiness

'Blessed . . . are those who hear the
word of God and obey it.'
Luke 11:28

He gives you strength to obey and
happiness as a reward.

Obedience = life

'I tell you the truth, if anyone keeps my word, he will never see death.'

John 8:51

Follow him here and he'll guide you all the way to your eternal home.

Easier said than done

'Love your enemies and pray for those who persecute you, that you may be sons of your Father in heaven.'

Matthew 5:44-45

Impossible with men, but possible through the grace of God.

And go the extra mile for them

'Love your enemies, do good to those who hate you, bless those who curse you, pray for those who ill-treat you. If someone strikes you on one cheek, turn to him the other also. If someone takes your cloak, do not stop him from taking your tunic. Give to everyone who asks you, and if anyone takes what belongs to you, do not demand it back.'

Luke 6:27-30

That's exactly what Jesus did for you when you were his enemy!

Pay attention to detail!

'Whoever can be trusted with very little can also be trusted with much, and whoever is dishonest with very little will also be dishonest with much.'
Luke 16:10

Little things matter!

Watch your tongue!
He's listening!

'But I tell you that men will have to give account on the day of judgement for every careless word they have spoken. For by your words you will be acquitted, and by your words you will be condemned.'

Matthew 12:36-37

Make sure you put your brain into gear before your tongue goes into action.

A firm foundation

'I will show you what he is like who comes to me and hears my words and puts them into practice. He is like a man building a house, who dug down deep and laid the foundation on rock. When the flood came, the torrent struck that house but could not shake it, because it was well built.'

Luke 6:47, 48

Are you building on sinking sand or solid rock?

Be proud to know him . . .

*'Whoever acknowledges me before men,
I will also acknowledge him before
my Father in heaven.'*
Matthew 10:32

. . . and he'll be proud to know you.

Don't be in love with the things of this world

'The man who loves his life will lose it, while the man who hates his life in this world will keep it for eternal life.'

John 12:25

Love the things of the Kingdom.

In the world, but not of it

'My prayer is not that you take them out of the world but that you protect them from the evil one. They are not of the world, even as I am not of it.'
John 17:15, 16

Jesus is praying that you will focus your thoughts and aims on the Kingdom.

You're not going it alone

*'I will talk to the Father, and he'll provide
you another Friend so that you will always
have someone with you. This Friend is
the Spirit of Truth. . . . he has been
staying with you, and will even be in you!'*
John 14:16, 17, MGE

Jesus has promised his Holy Spirit will
be your constant companion.

You can know the truth

'But when he, the Spirit of truth, comes,
he will guide you into all truth. He will not
speak on his own; he will speak only what he
hears, and he will tell you what is yet to come.'
John 16:13

Because God's gift of the Spirit will be
your indwelling guide.

The heart of the Gospel

'For God so loved the world that he gave his one and only Son, that whoever believes in him shall not perish but have eternal life. For God did not send his Son into the world to condemn the world, but to save the world through him.'

John 3:16, 17

Jesus said: 'I love you this much.'
And he stretched out his arms and died.

The Good Shepherd . . .

'If a man owns a hundred sheep, and one of them wanders away, will he not leave the ninety-nine on the hills and go to look for the one that wandered off? And if he finds it, I tell you the truth, he is happier about that one sheep than about the ninety-nine that did not wander off.'

Matthew 18:12, 13

. . . left Heaven to save *you*, his lost sheep.

Watch the Master

*'My command is this: Love each
other as I have loved you.'*
John 15:12

And copy his example.

If you love him . . .

'A new command I give you: Love one another. As I have loved you, so you must love one another. By this all men will know that you are my disciples, if you love one another.'

John 13:34-35

. . . then prove it by loving his other children.

The ultimate proof of love

'Greater love has no one than this, that he lay down his life for his friends.'

John 15:13

Jesus loved you so much he died for you.

A love without limits

'As the Father has loved me, so have I loved you. Now remain in my love.'

John 15:9

If he loves you that much, why would you want to separate yourself from him?

On intimate terms

*'I no longer call you servants, because a
servant does not know his master's business.
Instead, I have called you friends,
for everything that I learned from my
Father I have made known to you.'*
John 15:15

Just think of it! The King of the
universe calls *you* his friend!

He's not remote and far off

'I am the good shepherd; I know my sheep and my sheep know me.'

John 10:14

He's very near and knows you intimately.

The choice is yours

'Whoever believes in the Son has eternal life,
but whoever rejects the Son will not see life.'

John 3:36

Choose the Son and choose life.

Abundant life on offer

*'I have come that they may have life,
and have it to the full.'*

John 10:10

Why accept the poor imitation that the world
offers? Accept Jesus' offer of *real life* today.

Want to live forever?

'And this is the way to have eternal life – to know you, the only true God, and Jesus Christ, the one you sent to earth.'
John 17:3, NLT

Then get to know the only one who can make it possible.

A childlike faith is required

'I tell you the truth, anyone who will not receive the kingdom of God like a little child will never enter it.'
Mark 10:15

You have to exercise absolute trust in him.

Even a little faith goes a long way

'I tell you the truth, if you have faith as small as a mustard seed, you can say to this mountain, "Move from here to there" and it will move.'

Matthew 17:20

It only takes a little faith to move a mountain of difficulties.

He wasn't exaggerating

'Have faith in God, Jesus answered.
I tell you the truth, if anyone says to this
mountain, "Go, throw yourself into the sea,"
and does not doubt in his heart but
believes that what he says will happen,
it will be done for him.'
Mark 11:22-23

Pray God to give you a mountain-moving faith.

A prayer offered up in faith . . .

'Therefore I tell you, whatever you ask for in prayer, believe that you have received it, and it will be yours.'

Mark 11:24

. . . will be answered.

If you don't doubt . . .

'Everything is possible for him who believes.'
Mark 9:23

. . . anything is possible.

Divine Power there for the asking

'I tell you the truth, anyone who has faith in me will do what I have been doing. He will do even greater things than these, because I am going to the Father.'

John 14:12

Tap into that resource and watch what he can accomplish through you!

If you stay connected . . .

'If you remain in me and my words remain in you, ask whatever you wish, and it will be given you.'

John 15:7

You can be sure that your prayers will be heard.

Pray for strength

'Watch and pray so that you will not fall into temptation. The spirit is willing, but the body is weak.'

Matthew 26:41

Prayer can make you an overcomer.

Top of the prayer list

'If you then, though you are evil, know how to give good gifts to your children, how much more will your Father in heaven give the Holy Spirit to those who ask him!'
Luke 11:13

Ask God to give you an abundant presence of his richest gift.

Jesus has made a promise

'You may ask me for anything in my name, and I will do it.'

John 14:14

So ask!

Fullness of joy . . .

*'I tell you the truth, my Father will give you
whatever you ask in my name. . . . Ask and you
will receive, and your joy will be complete.'*
John 16:23, 24

. . . is yours for the asking.

Not the way of the world

'Instead, whoever wants to become great among you must be your servant, and whoever wants to be first must be slave of all.'

Mark 10:43-44

God's Kingdom has a topsy-turvy hierarchy!

Walk humbly before God . . .

'For everyone who exalts himself will be humbled, and he who humbles himself will be exalted.'

Luke 14:11

. . . and he will exalt you in due time.

Afraid?

'Why are you so afraid?
Do you still have no faith?'
Mark 4:40
'Don't be afraid; just believe.'
Mark 5:36

Why do we fear when the Creator of
the universe has promised to be with us
wherever we go and go before us
in whatever we do?

Nothing to fear

'Do not be afraid, little flock, for your Father has been pleased to give you the kingdom.'
Luke 12:32

You have the best Friend that Earth can afford, and one day Heaven will be yours.

Lonely?

'I will not leave you as orphans;
I will come to you.'
John 14:18

Your best Friend has promised never
to leave you alone.

Tired?

'Come with me by yourselves to a quiet place and get some rest.'

Mark 6:31

Jesus invites you to rest in him.

Troubled by sin?

*'Then neither do I condemn you, Jesus declared.
Go now and leave your life of sin.'*

John 8:11

'Therefore, there is now no condemnation for
those who are in Christ Jesus, . . .'

Romans 8:1

Abundant forgiveness is yours for the asking

'But the father said to his servants,
"Quick! Bring the best robe and put it on him.
Put a ring on his finger and sandals on his feet.
Bring the fattened calf and kill it. Let's
have a feast and celebrate. For this son of
mine was dead and is alive again; he was lost
and is found." So they began to celebrate.'

Luke 15:22-24

No recriminations – only celebrations!

The best invitation you'll ever have

'Are you tired? Worn out? Burned out on religion? Come to me. Get away with me and you'll recover your life. I'll show you how to take a real rest. Walk with me and work with me – watch how I do it. Learn the unforced rhythms of grace. I won't lay anything heavy or ill-fitting on you. Keep company with me and you'll learn to live freely and lightly.'

Matthew 11:28-30, MGE

It's an offer you can't afford to refuse.

An open invitation

'All that the Father gives me will come to me, and whoever comes to me I will never drive away.'

John 6:37

You're guaranteed acceptance.

You are of infinite value in Jesus' eyes . . .

'Are not two sparrows sold for a penny?
Yet not one of them will fall to the ground apart
from the will of your Father. And even the very hairs
of your head are all numbered. So don't be afraid;
you are worth more than many sparrows.'
Matthew 10: 29-31

. . . So valuable he thought you
were worth dying for.

Don't be afraid to ask . . .

'Ask and it will be given to you; seek and you will find; knock and the door will be opened to you. For everyone who asks receives; he who seeks finds; and to him who knocks, the door will be opened.'

Matthew 7:7-8

. . . You won't be disappointed if you do.

When the storms of life are raging . . .

'He got up, rebuked the wind and said to the waves, Quiet! Be still! Then the wind died down and it was completely calm.'

Mark 4:39

. . . let him whisper 'Peace, be still.'

Is your life fraught with anxiety and stress?

'Peace I leave with you; my peace I give you. I do not give to you as the world gives. Do not let your hearts be troubled and do not be afraid.'

John 14:27

Jesus offers you his peace – a gift that's out of this world.

Life getting on top of you?

'I have told you these things, so that in me you may have peace. In this world you will have trouble. But take heart! I have overcome the world.'
John 16:33

Rest in the peace he gives, and in his strength you can be an overcomer too!

'Lord, there are some things I just don't understand . . .'

'Jesus replied, You do not realise now what I am doing, but later you will understand.'
John 13:7

Jesus says, 'Just trust me for now, and one day everything will be clear to you.'

Weeping may endure for a night . . .

'I tell you the truth, you will weep and mourn while the world rejoices. You will grieve, but your grief will turn to joy.'

John 16:20

. . . but joy comes in the morning (Psalm 30:5).

Times may be hard now . . .

'A woman giving birth to a child has pain because her time has come; but when her baby is born she forgets the anguish because of her joy that a child is born into the world. So with you: Now is your time of grief, but I will see you again and you will rejoice, and no one will take away your joy.'
John 16:21, 22

. . . but look up, because better times are on the way.

Keep holding on – he's right by your side

'I know your deeds. See, I have placed before you an open door that no one can shut. I know that you have little strength, yet you have kept my word and have not denied my name. . . .
Since you have kept my command to endure patiently, I will also keep you from the hour of trial that is going to come upon the whole world to test those who live on the earth.
I am coming soon. Hold on to what you have, so that no one will take your crown.'

Revelation 3:8, 10, 11

The door to Heaven is wide open and victory is assured.

The most comforting words

'Do not let your hearts be troubled. Trust in God; trust also in me. In my Father's house are many rooms; if it were not so, I would have told you. I am going there to prepare a place for you. And if I go and prepare a place for you, I will come back and take you to be with me that you also may be where I am.'

John 14:1-3

Yes, Jesus is coming back for *you*.

The cataclysmic event of the ages

'At that time men will see the Son of Man coming in clouds with great power and glory. And he will send his angels and gather his elect from the four winds, from the ends of the earth to the ends of the heavens.'

Mark 13:26-27

There'll be no missing that event.

Be ready

'Be dressed ready for service and keep your lamps burning, like men waiting for their master to return from a wedding banquet, so that when he comes and knocks they can immediately open the door for him.'
Luke 12:35-36

And make sure you're wearing the wedding garment.

Ready or not, he's coming!

'For as lightning that comes from the east is visible even in the west, so will be the coming of the Son of Man.'

Matthew 24:27

And every eye shall see him.

You'd better believe it!

'I am the resurrection and the life. He who believes in me will live, even though he dies; and whoever lives and believes in me will never die.'

John 11:25-26

The Life-giver has promised to give *you* a share in eternal life.

Listen to him . . .

'I tell you the truth, whoever hears my word and believes him who sent me has eternal life and will not be condemned; he has crossed over from death to life.'

John 5:24

. . . and believe what he says and you're already halfway home.

Are you listening?

'I tell you the truth, a time is coming and has now come when the dead will hear the voice of the Son of God and those who hear will live.'
John 5:25

So listen and live!

He's coming with his reward

'My reward is with me, and I will give to everyone according to what he has done.'

Revelation 22:12

And his reward is everlasting happiness.

What really matters

'The Spirit gives life; the flesh counts for nothing. The words I have spoken to you are spirit and they are life.'
John 6:63

Jesus' words are life, so feed on them.

There's power in the Word

'Sanctify them by your truth. Your word is truth.'
John 17:17, NKJV

Power to change human hearts.

True freedom

'And you shall know the truth, and the truth shall make you free. . . . if the Son makes you free, you shall be free indeed.'
John 8:32, 36, NKJV

Trust him, follow him, and let him make you truly free.

Hang on in there!

'By standing firm you will gain life.'
'Staying with it – that's what is required.
Stay with it to the end. You won't
be sorry; you'll be saved.'
Luke 21:19, NIV, MGE

Staying power will bring rich rewards.

When weakness equals strength

'My grace is enough; it's all you need. My strength comes into its own in your weakness.'
2 Corinthians 12:9, MGE

Feel you can't make it? That's when Jesus can take over with his strength.

Tap into the Source of power

'Then Jesus came to them and said, All authority in heaven and on earth has been given to me.'
Matthew 28:18

Jesus has *all* authority. Don't you think he can sort out your problems and give you victory?

A Friend who'll never let you down

*'And surely I am with you always,
to the very end of the age.'*

Matthew 28:20

Yes, the One who has all authority is your
never-failing, ever-present Friend.

Jesus wants you to be with him

'Father, I want those you have given me to be with me where I am, and to see my glory, the glory you have given me because you loved me before the creation of the world.'

John 17:24

And he wants you to get to know him as he knows you.

He has a firm grip on you

'My sheep listen to my voice; I know them, and they follow me. I give them eternal life, and they shall never perish; no one can snatch them out of my hand.'

John 10:27, 28

And only *you* can loosen that grip.

A cause for rejoicing

'Rejoice because your names are written in heaven.'
Luke 10:20, NKJV

When you say Yes to Jesus, your name is on the heavenly register.

The great commission

*'Therefore go and make disciples of all
nations, baptising them in the name of the
Father and of the Son and of the Holy Spirit,
and teaching them to obey everything
I have commanded you.'*

Matthew 28:19-20

'As the Father has sent me, I am sending you.'

John 20:21

He sees and knows everything

'I know your deeds, your love and faith, your service and perseverance, and that you are now doing more than you did at first.'
Revelation 2:19

And your faithful service hasn't gone unnoticed.

Beautiful words

'Well done, good and faithful servant! You have been faithful with a few things; I will put you in charge of many things. Come and share your master's happiness!'

Matthew 25:23

Jesus sees your love for him, manifested in faithful service, and he has his welcome speech ready for when he greets you on that great day.

He was the Author of all things . . .

'I am the Alpha and the Omega, says the Lord God, who is, and who was, and who is to come, the Almighty.'
Revelation 1:8

. . . and he's the One who'll bring all things to their final consummation.

He has the keys!

*'Do not be afraid. I am the First and the Last.
I am the Living One; I was dead, and
behold I am alive for ever and ever! And I
hold the keys of death and Hades.'*
Revelation 1:17-18

Jesus has conquered death,
so you have nothing to fear.

Go and open the door!

'Here I am! I stand at the door and knock.
If anyone hears my voice and opens the door,
I will come in and eat with him, and he with me.
To him who overcomes, I will give the
right to sit with me on my throne, just as
I overcame and sat down with my
Father on his throne.'

Revelation 3:20-21

You'll never regret it.

He won't be long now

'Behold, I am coming soon! My reward is with me, and I will give to everyone according to what he has done. I am the Alpha and the Omega, the First and the Last, the Beginning and the End.'

Revelation 22:12, 13

And he's not coming empty-handed.

Good news that's worth repeating

'Yes, I am coming soon.'

'Amen. Come, Lord Jesus.'

Revelation 22:20

He said it; he meant it

*'Heaven and earth will pass away,
but my words will never pass away.'*
Matthew 24:35

So believe what he said and trust him.

When you believe in Jesus . . .

'I tell you the truth, he who believes has everlasting life.'

John 6:47

. . . eternal life begins **right here and now!**